The Why Overhead
© 2012, Adam Szymkowicz
Cover art by Original Works Publishing
First Printing, Trade Edition 2013
Printed in U.S.A.
ISBN 978-1-934962-80-0

More Great Plays Available From Original Works Publishing

THE ARCTIC CIRCLE
by Samantha Macher

3 Males, 2 Females

Synopsis: A Brechtian comedy about a woman in a troubled marriage who travels through time, space and Sweden to reexamine her past relationships for solutions to her newly found troubles. Unable to get the clear answers she needs, she must look inside herself to find what she is looking for.

THE JUNGLE FUN ROOM
by Brian Hampton

2 Males, 3 Females

Synopsis: The struggling actors of Jungle Fun Birthday Parties are preparing for Maddie's sixth birthday at the New York City Zoo. For Screg, Shelly, and Eve, it's just another day at work until Trevor, an eager new worker arrives, followed by Hillary Parker, the birthday girl's Oscar-winning mom. The result? A hilarious and emotional face-to-face with the past, present, and future—and a birthday party none of them will ever forget.

2

The Why Overhead

By Adam Szymkowicz

For those who make the day go by faster, especially Jodi Lipper, Michele Hammond and Joel Liestman.

The Why Overhead was first produced by Zootopia Theatre Co. It opened September 6, 2012 at the Access Theater in New York City.

Directed by Matthew J. Nichols
Set & Lighting Design: Andrew Lu
Costume Design: Caroline Berti
Sound Design: Brian Andrews
Original Music: Dru Cutler
Production Stage Manager: Phillip Rudy
Graphic Design: Aaron Hansen
Press Representative: Jonathan Slaff & Associates, www.jsnyc.com
Ticketing: Brown Paper Tickets

The Cast:

KAREN:	Heather Hollingsworth
DOG:	Larry Phillips
ALAN:	Scott Thomas
SAM:	Rowan Michael Meyer
SID:	Matthew Murumba
ANNIE:	Susan Louise O'Connor
NIGEL:	Jeffrey Emerson
DONALD:	David Bennett
VIOLET:	Cotton Wright
JESSICA:	Alexandra Hellquist
SUE:	Britney Burgess
MR. HENDERSON:	Ken Glickfeld

Special thanks to Matthew and Britney and the amazing cast and crew from the Zootopia production. Thanks also Kristen Palmer, John and Rhoda Szymkowicz, Tish Dace, Travis York, Flux Theater Ensemble, Larry Kunofsky and Purple Rep, and the actors from the serials series—Piper Gunnarson Bishop, Drew Hirshfield, Dana Jacks, Brian Pracht, Christina Shipp and Christopher T. VanDijk. This play would not have been possible had I not spent many hours in offices. So thank you to the folks at Randstad in New York and Prostaff in Minneapolis and of course, everyone at the development office at The Columbia University School of Journalism.

CHARACTERS

KAREN
DOG
ALAN
SAM
SID
ANNIE
NIGEL
DONALD
VIOLET
JESSICA
SUE
MR. HENDERSON

(There is no doubling except everyone will be a hobo)

NOTE: More POLICE OFFICERS can come in with SUE and stand around taking notes at the end if you want. But they are not necessary. It all depends on the size of your stage and if you have people who want to do this.

PLACE

New York City—

An office, KAREN's apartment, DONALD's apartment, a street.

THE WHY OVERHEAD

1

8:11 AM

(KAREN and her DOG in their apartment. KAREN wears pajamas or a robe.)

KAREN: *(to her DOG)* I see you looking at me. I know what you're thinking. You're thinking I should get dressed and go to work. "Get going," your eyes say. But I am moving. You might not see it, but I'm moving. It's slow sure, but I'm faster than erosion. Faster than continental drift. But wait a minute. Let me rest. What's the hurry? Live in the moment here with me. I'm here right now and I aim to stay here for another few minutes, an hour, a day. Everything will go on without me. I didn't go to work yesterday or the day before and yet the world continues to revolve. New York does not need me. People go about their lives. No one calls to ask where I am. It's like I don't exist at all. But I do exist don't I?

DOG: Ruff!

KAREN: Your mouth says yes but your eyes say no. Please stop judging me. I don't need to go to work, not today. It won't affect the food in your dish. You'll get fed. And you won't be lonely.

DOG: Ruff.

KAREN: Please don't say anything. I know you disapprove and I hear you but it's really not what I want right now and I know you subscribe to a sort of tough love viewpoint, but sometimes that's not very helpful and furthermore, not appreciated. Don't look at me like that. I do appreciate you, just not the hard line you try to draw sometimes. The world is not black and white. And colors can be confusing, so let me sit and rest and figure out a few things, okay? It'll be fun. I can stay here all day with you. We can watch bad romantic comedies and you can jump up on the bed and curl up with me and we can eat crackers if we want. I won't kick you out. And tomorrow? *(beat)* Who knows? Let's just think of today. Everything is so uncertain these days.

(Pause)

DOG: Ruff!

9:23 AM

(At the office, cubicles. Phones ringing. Sounds of a fax machine, typing.)

SID: *(on phone)* Yes, Ma'am. No, Ma'am. We'll get that right out to you. Thank you for calling. We're here from nine a.m. to five p.m. Monday through—*(the woman has hung up.)* Okay then.

SAM: *(peers his head over the cubicle)* What's the dare for the day?

SID: Oh, man, I don't know.

SAM: ALAN! ALAN! ALAN! ALAN! I think he's here. ALAN! ALAN! ALAN! ALAN!!! ALAN!!!!

(ALAN appears.)

ALAN: What?

SAM: What do you got for today?

ALAN: Um…

SID: What do ya got?

SAM: You got one?

ALAN: Hold on. Yeah. Okay.

SID: What do ya got?

ALAN: Right before they hang up, you say real quick, "I love you."

SAM: That's funny.

SID: "Thank you for calling, I love you."

SAM: "I love you, sir."

ALAN: Yeah.

SAM: Dare accepted.

SID: Accepted.

ALAN: Accepted.

SAM: Good work.

ALAN: Thanks.

(Enter NIGEL.)

NIGEL: Where the fuck is Karen?

SAM: I don't know.

SID: Well, if she's not coming to work again, I'm going to stop working. I'm serious. If she's not working, we shouldn't have to.

NIGEL: Yeah, Okay.

(NIGEL exits to his desk.)

ALAN: She might come in, still.

SAM: Has anyone heard from her? Hey! Has anyone heard from Karen!

ANNIE, NIGEL, ALAN, SID, JESSICA: (off) *(From various parts of the office)* No!

ALAN: Maybe she called in sick to Mr. Henderson.

(ANNIE comes over.)

ANNIE: I mean at the very least she could send us an email.

SID: She probably died.

ANNIE: Stop.

SID: She probably fell off her treadmill.

ALAN: Fell to her death off the treadmill?

SID: Yeah fell to her death. That dog of hers is probably eating her right now.

ANNIE: Stop.

SID: Well, I'm not doing any work until she comes back. If my boss can play hooky, so can I.

3

9:24 AM

(KAREN and her DOG in their apartment.)

KAREN: Here's the thing, Eugene.

DOG: Ruff.

KAREN: I know you think I'm crazy, but I woke up one day and there was a *why* hanging over everything I did all day. Why? What for? How come? It kept poking at me, insistently. Why! Why? And I didn't have an answer, you know? I was doing the things I thought I was supposed to do even though I hated doing them. And really, I don't have a good reason for doing any of these things. And so it stayed. That big *WHY* hanging over my head, over my life and it's coloring everything. And I have no answer. I don't know why. Why? Why am I doing anything? So I decided from now on not to do anything unless I had a damn good reason. So let's keep watching this film, because it makes me feel good and it takes me away. And I'll keep petting you because you like it and I like how soft you are.

DOG: Okay, but what if you never have a good reason to do anything ever again? Will you just drop out of life altogether, and if so, what will that look like?

KAREN: That's a good question. Why don't we both think about that, maybe after the film is over. Okay?

DOG: Ruff.

KAREN: Okay.

4

10:45 AM

(NIGEL is working on his computer in his cubicle. AN-NIE can be heard in another part of the stage.)

ANNIE: Who left this in the refrigerator? Oh my god!

(ANNIE enters NIGEL's area carrying a brown paper bag. It looks wet, like it may have leaked.)

ANNIE: Is this yours?

NIGEL: What's that smell?

ANNIE: It's yours, isn't it?

NIGEL: Get that thing away from me!

ANNIE: You can't just leave smelly shit in the refrigerator just because you don't want to touch it. You have to take responsibility for the stenches you create, Nigel.

NIGEL: It's not mine.

ANNIE: It's not yours?

NIGEL: It's not mine.

ANNIE: This isn't yours?

NIGEL: No.

ANNIE: It's not?

NIGEL: No.

ANNIE: Whose is it?

NIGEL: How should I know?

ANNIE: If it's not yours, whose is it?

NIGEL: I don't know. Maybe you shouldn't bring me every smelly thing you find hanging around.

ANNIE: I wouldn't except that every time there's something that smells it seems to belong to you.

NIGEL: How about your smelly feet and your smelly face?

ANNIE: My what? How about I shove this bag down your throat!?

NIGEL: Go ahead and try it, hot shot!

ANNIE: You are so asking for it.

NIGEL: Are you going to give it to me?

ANNIE: I would so kick your ass.

NIGEL: You are a wimpy little girl.

ANNIE: You are a wimpier littler girl.

(With that, she throws the paper bag on his desk.)

NIGEL: Oh, come on! Come on! Foul! I call foul!

(But ANNIE has left.)

NIGEL: You better run. You better be afraid of me. I am a man. I am a big man and I won't take this kind of insanity from a girl like you! I have scaled mountains. I have forged rivers. I have run in races. I built snow caves and spent the night in them. You hear me?! I jumped out of airplanes. I drove a motorcycle. I am very hairy. I work out two or three times a week. With free weights. I eat lots of vegetables. I am a fairly good pool player. Also pinochle. I could catch a tiger if I had the right equipment and enough time on my hands and if I was in the vicinity of tigers. I have a charming personality. I can make up jokes that people repeat later and don't even realize they're mine. I can make intricate cages out of popsicle sticks. My chest is enormous! I am a wealth of knowledge about music and musicians, especially in the years nineteen fifty nine to nineteen ninety-four. I write poetry. I won an award once for punctuality. My smile is terrific. I used to be a choir boy. I can peel oranges with great speed and dexterity. I am good at choosing shoes. I once played tennis for three hours. I am omnipotent! Okay, well maybe that last one isn't true. But I am a man and I will crush you. You hear me?! YOU HEAR ME?!!

SAM: I hear you and I want you to shut up.

16

5

10:47 AM

(At DONALD's apartment, DONALD talks to a stuffed cat. No, not like a stuffed animal. Like a cat that used to be alive that was taken to the taxidermist and was stuffed and now sits lifelike before us. The cat meows, yet eerily, the sound does not seem to come from the cat. DONALD can meow for the CAT if you like.)

CAT: Meow.

DONALD: What's that mittens?

CAT: *(Louder)* Meow.

DONALD: Oh. No. no. Don't worry about me. It's true I've been a bit sulky since that female laid me off. But I'm recovering, licking my wounds. Anyway, I have ideas about how to take care of that.

CAT: Meow?

DONALD: Sure, I might apply for some jobs in my sector. That could be part of the plan. But that's not the main plan.

CAT: Meow.

DONALD: Well, I'm glad you asked. You see, I have not been true to my nature. My nature is murder and pillaging. My nature is smash and grab and instead I had meetings a lot and typed things into Excel documents. I should be harpooning seals and drinking the blood of my enemies, not filling out requisitions for erasers.   (continued)

17

DONALD (Cont'd): So the job was not in fact a good match. Still, for them to treat me so discourteously, well I'm going to take care of that. Don't worry.

CAT: Meow.

DONALD: Don't worry about that. Don't worry just yet. Just know I'm working it out. I mean, she should have laid off one of those worthless cabana boys or one of those phone jockeys. I was the office manager! You can't go on without an office manager. I don't know what she was thinking. The place is probably falling apart without me at the helm, ordering the paper. Answering the phones. Keeping track of the sick days and the personal days. *(beat)* Maybe I should poison her dog.

CAT: Meow.

DONALD: You like that idea, huh?

CAT: Meow.

DONALD: Me too. But I don't know where she lives. She's unlisted, you see. Anyway, it seems unfair to hurt an animal who has nothing to do with her. But it would hurt her a great deal. It's a tough decision. Life is full of tough decisions. But I have a better idea anyway. I may as well tell you. I've been keeping it to myself. You know what I'm going to do?

CAT: Meow?

(DONALD whispers something to CAT.)

CAT: Meow.

6

10:54 AM

(ALAN approaches JESSICA's cube.)

ALAN: Oh, hey, Jessica, I didn't hear you come back.

JESSICA: Yeah.

ALAN: How was the dentist?

JESSICA: Fine.

(SID enters.)

SID: Hi, Jessica.

JESSICA: Hi.

SID: How was the dentist?

JESSICA: Fine.

SID: I bet you look really cute with gauze in your mouth.

JESSICA: Yes, I do.

ALAN: Did you have any cavities?

JESSICA: No.

SID: She has perfect teeth. Look at those teeth. That girl doesn't have cavities.

JESSICA: I don't have cavities.

ALAN: Maybe she doesn't have a sweet tooth.

JESSICA: I have a sweet tooth. It's just I brush is all.

SID: She brushes.

JESSICA: And floss.

SID: She flosses.

JESSICA: And mouthwash.

SID: She m—

ALAN: Shut up. You're making a fool of yourself.

SID: No, I'm not. Am I?

JESSICA: I wasn't paying attention.

SID: See?

ALAN: She's not paying attention to you because you're a fool.

SID: I am not a fool. You are the fool, fool. Anyway, what do you care?

ALAN: I don't.

SID: Good.

ALAN: Fine.

JESSICA: Um. Do you want something? Or are you just going to hang around my cube and argue.

ALAN: Oh, actually . . . So you want to—

SID: Okay, yeah.

ALAN: Should I ask or—

SID: You can ask.

ALAN: All right.

SID: Or I could ask.

ALAN: Okay.

SID: Or we could both.

ALAN: So Jessica...

JESSICA: Yeah?

SID: We wanted to ask you—

JESSICA: I'm not having a threesome with you.

ALAN: No, no. We weren't going to ask that.

SID: We don't want that. Trust me.

ALAN: No.

SID: I mean, he might, but I don't. Not that I don't want to get in on with you, but I just don't want anyone else involved, you know?

JESSICA: What do you want?

SID: Right.

ALAN: Well, when are you going to lunch today?

JESSICA: I'm busy. For lunch. I'm not having lunch with you.

SID: Oh, no.

ALAN: We didn't mean that.

SID: No.

ALAN: We have a surprise, but we need access to your cube to make it happen and we need you to be away, for like an hour.

SID: An hour?

ALAN: Yeah, bout an hour.

SID: Make it an hour fifteen.

JESSICA: Fine.

ALAN: What time?

JESSICA: One.

SID: Perfect.

ALAN: Great!

(They stand there, smiling at her.)

JESSICA: Okay, now go away so I can do work.

SID: Right.

ALAN: Okay.

SID: See you at one.

(They exit. SID looks back one last time and smiles.)

7

11:15 AM

(At SAM's desk. His phone rings. He puts on his headset.)

SAM: Thank you for calling customer service. This is Sam. How may I help you today?

(Lights up on VIOLET in another part of the stage. Where is she? In her house, on the street?)

VIOLET: Hello, Sam.

SAM: Oh, hello. It's you.

VIOLET: Yes.

SAM: I was hoping you'd call.

VIOLET: You knew I would.

SAM: I know. But I didn't know when. It's like a treat. And a surprise.

VIOLET: Am I a treat and a surprise?

SAM: You are. You really are. So how are you doing?

VIOLET: I'm good.

SAM: I love your voice.

VIOLET: Thank you.

SAM: I got those pictures you sent.

VIOLET: Yeah?

SAM: You are so fricking cute. And beautiful too, you know. You are cute but at the same time gorgeous.

VIOLET: Thank you.

SAM: And hot too. I don't want you to think just because you're a great beauty you're not sizzling hot too.

VIOLET: Thank you. I liked your photos too.

SAM: You did?

VIOLET: They were funny.

SAM: I was trying to entertain you, you know.

VIOLET: You have really nice eyes.

SAM: Thanks. I was born with them. I mean, they've gotten bigger, but they're the ones I've always had.

VIOLET: Lovely.

SAM: Lovely, huh?

VIOLET: Don't embarrass me.

SAM: I'm not.

VIOLET: Did you ever think you'd get along so well with someone calling in one day with a warranty question?

SAM: Never. I never thought work would bring me such pleasure.

VIOLET: It's a special thing. Nothing like this ever happened to me.

SAM: Me either. I'm so glad you took a chance.

VIOLET: Me too. It was a lark.

SAM: I'm glad.

VIOLET: I don't do things like that.

SAM: No.

VIOLET: Except that once.

SAM: Yeah. When can we meet?

VIOLET: Face to face?

SAM: Yeah.

VIOLET: I don't know.

SAM: What do you mean?

VIOLET: Timing is really important. We can't do it too soon and we can't wait too long.

SAM: Okay, so when?

VIOLET: *(looking at her watch.)* Oh shit. I got to go to work. I'll call you back.

SAM: Okay. Call me back.

SID: *(on the phone.)*   Okay, ma'am. Have a nice day.
     (beat) I love you.

(SID and ALAN laugh.)

8

11:25 AM

(At KAREN's apartment. A movie has just ended. Maybe KAREN is crying a little. The DOG is not.)

KAREN: That was a gorgeous film.

DOG: It was okay.

KAREN: I thought it was touching. Did you see his face when he saw her there at the end?

DOG: I have a hard time seeing two dimensional images. Also I'm near sighted.

KAREN: We should get you glasses.

DOG: Okay. So we've seen that movie. Now what? Are you going to continue this? You want to watch another movie? And then another? You want to delay your life indefinitely and never get dressed?

KAREN: Oh, Doggy. You really don't let me collect myself.

DOG: You've been collecting yourself for a week. I demand decisions. I don't want you to go through life like this.

KAREN: I know you don't.

DOG: It's okay for me. Because I'm a dog.

KAREN: I know. That's unfair.

DOG: Of course it is. But I'm a dog and you aren't. You can't just become a dog. One of us has to be the human.

KAREN: I guess.

DOG: And it's not going to be me.

KAREN: Okay.

DOG: So?

KAREN: I have one idea.

DOG: Let's hear it.

KAREN: Here is what I propose. I take you for a walk. But then we keep walking. We take a walk that lasts for the rest of our lives. I pack up all the food and necessities. We go off with a tent and we walk the length and breadth of the United States for the rest of our lives.

DOG: Like hobos?

KAREN: Like free people.

DOG: Will we bring the TV?

KAREN: I don't think we can.

DOG: I'm in.

KAREN: Okay. Let's pack.

DOG: Wait. This means no more city, no more job, no more walks in the park. No more treats from the high class pet store.

KAREN: Yes but it means lots more cities, and fields and woods and streams. It means chasing rabbits sometimes. There are the possibilities of other jobs. Someday we may stop and stay somewhere else for a while. But yes it means casting off our old life for the unknown, for a new life, for adventure.

DOG: There will be new smells.

KAREN: Yes.

DOG: I like that.

KAREN: We are agreed?

DOG: Okay.

KAREN: Okay?

DOG: I think. Let me think. Let me just mull it over.

KAREN: You're afraid.

DOG: Just give me a minute.

KAREN: Okay.

DOG: Ruff.

9

12:13 PM

(ANNIE at her cubical, maybe offstage. NIGEL at his cube.)

ANNIE: What the? Is this cottage cheese?

(ANNIE screams, then runs over to NIGEL's area.)

ANNIE: Did you put spread cottage cheese on my desk?

NIGEL: Was it large curd?

ANNIE: Yes.

NIGEL: Two percent?

ANNIE: I don't know.

NIGEL: Because I did put two percent, large curd cottage cheese all over your desk. If that is what you're referring to, yes, that was me.

ANNIE: Fucking—

NIGEL: I think it's yours actually.

ANNIE: Mine!

NIGEL: Someone left it in the fridge to go sour. I see you eating cottage cheese an awful lot. And you know, it had your name on it, so…

ANNIE: You are an asshole.

NIGEL: Does it smell bad?

ANNIE: You're disgusting!

NIGEL: Well, you made my desk smell bad.

ANNIE: That's not the same thing.

NIGEL: I refuse to be bullied by you anymore!

ANNIE: You realize what this means, don't you?

NIGEL: That you're going to apologize?

ANNIE: This time you went too far. This time, you have stepped over the line, Nigel Melnick.

NIGEL: Good.

ANNIE: This means war!

NIGEL: Bring your war. I welcome it. I will defeat you soundly. Bring whatever you have. Your pathetic intellect and weak muscles are no match for me. I will crush you.

ANNIE: We'll see who crushes who.

NIGEL: I will crush you!

(ANNIE exits. JESSICA walks over wearing headphones. She takes them off as she approaches NIGEL.)

JESSICA: Do you understand the filing system?

NIGEL: I am going to crush her.

JESSICA: Can you explain the filing system to me?

NIGEL: No, I don't know.

JESSICA: I don't know what the fuck Donald did. It's not alphabetical and it's not numerical and I can't figure out what it is.

NIGEL: Yeah I don't know. Maybe Karen knows.

JESSICA: She hasn't been here all week.

NIGEL: Oh. Right.

JESSICA: You don't think . . .

NIGEL: What?

JESSICA: Donald did something to Karen.

NIGEL: No. No. I don't think so. Will you leave me alone, now? I have to plot Annie's demise.

JESSICA: Oh, Okay.

(JESSICA puts her headphones on and starts to walk away as SAM enters.)

SAM: Hey does anyone understand the filing system? Hey. Jessica? Nigel? Hey. Hey! Why is everyone ignoring me?

12:52 PM

(SID and ALAN enter JESSICA's area carrying step ladders.)

SID: Hi, Jessica.

ALAN: Hi, Jessica.

JESSICA: What's with the ladders?

ALAN: It's part of the surprise.

JESSICA: And I'm going to like this?

SID: We think so.

JESSICA: And you need ladders?

ALAN: We do.

JESSICA: Is it dangerous, this thing you're doing? Does it have the potential to fall on me?

SID: We don't think so.

JESSICA: I just don't want things to fall on me. The last apartment I had, the ceiling was falling on me, piece by piece.

ALAN: Right. You told us about this.

JESSICA: Little crumbs at first but then bigger and bigger chunks of plaster, just raining down. I had to fall asleep holding an umbrella over my head. I'm glad I don't live there anymore. It was a nightmare. Whenever the people above me were having sex it was like it was snowing. You're not going to make it snow on me?

ALAN: No.

JESSICA: Good. I hate snow. I should move to LA. Do you think I'm attractive enough for LA?

SID: Absolutely.

ALAN: No doubt.

SID: Wait, you hate snow?

JESSICA: Yeah.

SID: Really?

JESSICA: Yeah. Rain too. Anything that falls.

ALAN: We won't make it snow.

JESSICA: And nothing will fall on me, right?

ALAN: Right.

SID: Right. Quite the opposite, actually.

JESSICA: Because I can't handle things falling on my head. My older brother when I was a kid, used to drop things on me. He would pin me to the ground and then drop things on my face. Gummi Bears, ping pong balls, chocolate chips, our goldfish.

SID: Your goldfish?

JESSICA: Legos, Barbie heads, pens, popsicles, water balloons, eggs, tin foil, socks, shoes, magnets, pieces of paper, jello, cereal, the cat.

ALAN: Really?

JESSICA: Marshmallows, a slinky, legos. Flowers, ice, a recorder, matches, unlit. Matches, lit. matchbox cars, cellophane, statue of the virgin Mary, chapstick, butter, and then liquids. Juice, milk, water of course. Salt, pepper, thyme, rosemary, parsley, bacon bits, tongue depressors, spit, oregano, pancakes, stuffed animals, marbles, lettuce, sticks, forks, spoons, wood chips, chopsticks, erasers. Legos. Did I say legos? Toast, rubber balls, hackey sacks, Frisbees, action figures, dirt, spare change, mints, catfish.

ALAN: Catfish?

JESSICA: It is my dream to someday lock him in a room, handcuff him to a chair and spend all day and night dumping things over his head.

ALAN: Huh.

SID: Yeah, we won't drop anything on you.

JESSICA: Okay, good. I'll be back in an hour.

(Exit JESSICA, carrying an umbrella.)

SID: Okay.

ALAN: Oh, wait. Make it an hour fifteen. Jessica!

SID: She's gone.

ALAN: Okay. *(Pause.)* Before we start, I want to be clear.

SID: Okay, let's be clear.

ALAN: I'm only teaming up with you on this because I think you know what you're doing and I care about the structural integrity of the design. We'll do it together and it will be great and we will perhaps both benefit. But after this is over, it's every man for himself, again.

SID: Agreed.

ANNIE: Does anyone have any paper? Are we out of paper? *(Pause.)* Does anyone know how to order paper?

11

1:18 PM

(SAM at his desk on the phone. VIOLET on her cell, wherever VIOLET is.)

SAM: It's great to hear your voice.

VIOLET: Yours too.

SAM: And I love this relationship.

VIOLET: I love it too.

SAM: This phone thing.

VIOLET: Yeah.

SAM: It's great. You know I haven't even told anyone about it?

VIOLET: Really?

SAM: Not that I don't want to and not because I'm worried if I speak of it, it will cease to exist or something, but because I want it just for me.

VIOLET: Oh.

SAM: Other people might not understand. And they'll define it and then their definition will limit it. And right now, it's limitless.

VIOLET: Oh. That's nice.

SAM: So is this. That's what I'm saying.

VIOLET: I agree.

SAM: But we will meet, won't we?

VIOLET: Of course. It's just.

SAM: The timing.

VIOLET: Right. You have to get these things right.

SAM: I guess.

VIOLET: I'm still newly out of a relationship.

SAM: Right.

VIOLET: I'm just not sure I'm ready to take on another one. Not with the kind of attention I think a relationship like ours would deserve.

SAM: Yeah.

VIOLET: My parents grew up in the same town. They knew each other since the sixth grade. And my father was in love with my mother from the first moment they met, but even though he was there the entire time she was growing up she never really saw him. She didn't see him until eight years later when they both ended up taking a semester abroad at the same time from their different colleges. They were both Americans in Prague and they found each other one night in a smoky bar and my mom fell in love with him over Czech beer.

(continued)

VIOLET (Cont'd): And he had never stopped being in love with her. And six months later they were married. So you see, timing is very important. Sometimes things have to happen when they happen, not when we want them to happen. You know?

SAM: I guess.

VIOLET: So you'll wait.

SAM: I guess. I mean, it has to be this way? You're sure. Cause I'm just not sure.

VIOLET: Listen, I got to be across town, but I'll call you later, Okay?

SAM: Okay. Wait.

VIOLET: What?

SAM: No, nevermind.

VIOLET: Bye.

SAM: Wait.

VIOLET: What?

SAM: Nothing. Nothing. Bye.

VIOLET: Bye.

(SAM hangs up. ANNIE is standing in his cubicle.)

SAM: What?

ANNIE: You got a girlfriend?

SAM: No.

ANNIE: It's okay if you have a girlfriend.

SAM: I don't.

ANNIE: It's okay if you do.

SAM: It's not that yet.

ANNIE: All right.

SAM: Not yet.

ANNIE: Fine. *(beat)* I had a girlfriend once.

SAM: You did?

ANNIE: It didn't last. There was something untrue about it for me.

SAM: Oh.

ANNIE: It's boys for me. For always. But lately, nothing.

SAM: Huh.

ANNIE: Bone dry.

SAM: Oh.

ANNIE: I've become a fighter instead of a lover, I think. There was a fork in the road and I took the fighter path and I didn't turn back. Every relationship since then has been about being right. I'm not quite sure why. I don't think I'm a particular right person but get me in a room with someone I'm dating and suddenly I'm Encyclopedia Annie. What the fuck is that about?

SAM: I don't know.

ANNIE: Every little thing any of my exes has ever done makes me want to destroy them. I look at their stupid faces and I want to ruin them. Is that love?

SAM: Probably not.

ANNIE: If it is, it's a pernicious kind of love. Why do I want to destroy things that I love, that love me? If we hadn't been born with opposable thumbs all those years ago, we would have been killed off by tigers or something before we got smart enough to make clubs or guns or nuclear weapons. I wish I had a club right now. I would bash Nigel's head in with it. *(beat)* I need coffee.

(ANNIE walks away.)

SAM: Okay, nice talking to you.

1:22 PM

(DONALD and his CAT.)

DONALD: Mittens?

CAT: Meow.

DONALD: I finished it finally. My manifesto. You want to hear it?

CAT: Meow.

DONALD: Oh good. I was hoping you'd want to hear it. Are you ready? Are you comfortable?

CAT: Meow.

DONALD: "Manifesto to leave behind after everything has happened to explain why in case it is less than obvious." Is that title too long?

CAT: Meow.

DONALD: Yeah I don't think so either. *(DONALD clears his throat.)* "There are certain times in history when certain actions become necessary. Right now it is a time when there are great inequalities. I have taken on the responsibility to right wrongs to stop injustice and to use the pen here and later the sword so that the words from my pen will be read. Anyone can write anything, but you also have to get people to read what you write.   (continued)

DONALD (Cont'd): That's what the sword is for. I stand before you a man ready to take drastic actions. There are men that take actions and men that do nothing but complain. We are all angry but only the brave few who stand up and fight back will be able to accomplish anything of note. History will show that my actions were the right actions at the right time. History will record today as the turning point for America when a wave of citizens led by me took back their country."

"I ask that in my absence, one of my future followers take care of my cat Mittens. She needs neither food nor water. She has evolved beyond life. She only requires company and for someone to talk to her and listen to her. I know that Mittens and I will see each other in the next life and I wouldn't be surprised if she became a conduit for my messages from beyond the grave. In the past, I have spoken to many great leaders through her. Like Marie Antoinette, John Adams, Martin Van Buren, Henry Ford, and a spirit guide dog named Hamish. So when you need to reach me, ask Mittens nicely and I'm sure she will oblige. And through her I will give you future guidance on how to overthrow the government and corporations and create a civilization for the people by the people. The right people, that is."

"In conclusion, when statues of me are built, I ask that Mittens be portrayed as well in bronze or gold or whatever. Her guidance has been incredibly helpful and without her I couldn't have accomplished what my actions accomplished. Like the straw that breaks the camel's back, the small deeds of today will reverberate for generations."

"I sign this with my left hand though I am right handed." And then I signed it. Do you like it?

CAT: *(weird echoing meow.)* Meow.

DONALD: Me too.

13

1:32 PM

(SID and ALAN are both on ladders constructing something over JESSICA's cubicle. It's hard to tell what it is they're building at this point.)

SID: I'm just saying it's clear that she and I have a strong connection and I think you should just step aside and let nature take its course.

ALAN: I should step aside.

SID: You should step aside.

ALAN: I don't think so, Sid. First of all, you don't have some kind of special relationship with her. You just don't. You're imagining things. Second of all, you're just not as physically attractive as me.

SID: What? You're dog-like in appearance, while I am sculpted. Additionally, you are not funny. I am very funny and she loves that about me.

ALAN: I've never heard you be funny.

SID: I'm funny all the time.

ALAN: Because you tell knock knock jokes?

SID: I am inherently funny.

ALAN: You're inherently goofy. I'm not sure that's the same thing. I mean if she's looking for a clown, I mean strictly a non-funny clown, maybe you'd do okay, but if she wants a life full of joy, I'm not sure you'd be the first choice.

SID: I am full of joy.

ALAN: When it comes down to it, you're just not cool. I'm much cooler than you.

SID: I don't think you're cool.

ALAN: Well, look at the crowd you run with. Would you know cool if you saw it? I mean I think some people like you can never be cool because you don't understand what it is. I, however, am very aware of cool and have been cool since puberty. That's just how I roll.

SID: Bullshit. That's what I say.

ALAN: Whatever. Jessica knows. I vibrate cool and she wants to rub up against that shit.

SID: She doesn't want anything to do with you and if you left us alone for more than five minutes you'd see that because we'd be making out.

ALAN: Really?

SID: Really. She's just waiting to get me alone. But you can't take a hint. So I'm here to tell you. Step back, cool kid. No one wants your vibrations.

ALAN: Whatever. If she was into you, you two would have gone on a date by now.

SID: She and I don't think that we should mix our work lives and social lives. It's not professional.

ALAN: Well, then I don't think you're going to be making out with her.

SID: Not yet, I mean. We have to discover that we can't live without each other and then, human resources be damned!

ALAN: Yeah, okay.

SID: Yeah.

ALAN: New dare. The first one that gets a date with her wins.

SID: Really?

ALAN: Put up or shut up.

SID: Dare accepted.

ALAN: Accepted.

SID: You are so going down.

ALAN: You know what? If you had the opportunity, you wouldn't even know what to do with a girl like Jessica. She would intimidate you.

SID: Me? No way. The first thing I would do is make sweet love to her.

ALAN: That's the first thing you would do? No dinner?

SID: Oh. Yeah. We would have dinner at an extravagant restaurant. Then we would go see a film, probably something foreign. Then I would take her dancing. Followed by ice skating, dog racing, the opera, a baseball game, a long walk in the park, a trip to a museum, perhaps the MOMA. If it's hot out, we'd sneak into a hotel pool. Then we'd sit in the back garden of a Brooklyn restaurant and drink mimosas.

ALAN: Mimosas?

SID: Margaritas. Long Island iced tea. Or tequila. A full bottle at the table and two shot glasses. And big glasses of ice water.

ALAN: Okay.

SID: Then we would go back to my place and make love.

ALAN: I mean that sounds like an okay date. For someone like you who has no imagination.

SID: What would be your date?

ALAN: I would pick her up in a horse drawn carriage.

SID: One of those dumb things at the park always shitting on the street?

ALAN: I would have a bouquet of red roses for her at her door. She would blush. Kiss me sweetly on the cheek.

SID: Strictly platonic.

ALAN: At first. But we would ride the horse-drawn carriage through the park at night.

SID: Just like tourists.

ALAN: Then dinner and drinks and a show. She's always loved Broadway musicals. I'd take her to something light and funny. But there would be that seduction scene. What is a musical without a seduction scene? And when the scene begins I will kiss her softly on the neck and then when she murmurs her appreciation, I would begin to bite a little bit then a little more until most of her neck is in my mouth. It is at this moment that she feels the intensity of my lust and is turned on by my complete and utter power over her. I put one arm around her waist, and grasp the divot under her knee, with my hand. My thumb on top. And I would pick her up and carry her from the theatre. We would hail a cab. Our clothes are already disheveled when the cab arrives and we start our lovemaking in the backseat. We just can't wait. We're too caught up. And then when we get back to my place, we do it again. And again and again.

SID: Classy.

ALAN: I don't expect you to understand. A woman like Jessica needs to be devoured with a hunger reserved the finest things in life.

SID: The best food in the world is in front of you and you want to inhale it. You're trying to do a keg-stand with a Chateau Margot.

ALAN: Whatever. I don't have to justify myself to you.
When she picks me over you, you'll see.

SID: So never, then.

ALAN: You'll see.

14

2:01 PM

(In KAREN's apartment, KAREN puts on a giant back-pack. It is normal backpack width for backpacking but is much much taller. It is probably twice her height before she even puts it on her back. There is a sleeping bag on top and what is probably a tent on the bottom and lots of things hanging off it like pots and pans and boots.)

KAREN: *(unfolding a map.)* So what I think is, we walk north, take the G.W. Bridge to Jersey and then keep walking across the country seeking adventure and odd jobs. We camp on the side of the roads and we steal apples from trees and tomatoes from vegetable gardens. Some nights we sleep under the stars, other nights in the tent or in people's barns or under billboards. Or we stowaway on trains and ride the rails.

DOG: Are we hobos?

KAREN: I don't know. Do you want to be a hobo?

DOG: It doesn't matter to me. Are there hobo songs we can sing?

KAREN: I'm sure there are. We can learn them on the road. You ready?

DOG: Before we do this, has this been thought out? I'm not a complainer. I don't care where I sleep. I'm just a dog. My needs are simple. I just wonder about leaving behind the warm rooms and the kitchen and couch and things.

KAREN: We don't need these things. These things are enslaving us. We don't need too much comfort. We don't need to live so close to everyone else so that we hear them breathe. We need not be awoken by car alarms or drunken shouting or loud sex. Instead, we will have freedom. Our only neighbors will be fellow travelers on the open road.

DOG: Are you sure? This means no more health insurance.

KAREN: Health insurance is so bourgeois.

DOG: Most of the time I'll be the only one you will be talking to for hours and hours, days maybe. You're going from eight million people to one dog. Are you okay with that?

KAREN: I think so. I want some time to think, some space to breathe.

DOG: Some hobo songs to sing?

KAREN: Sure.

DOG: Okay then. Do you have the dog bowl?

KAREN: Got it! I'll need to put a leash on you. At least until we leave New York.

DOG: Grrr.

(He lets her put a leash on him.)

KAREN: I know. Freedom can be tricky like that. Well, I guess this is it. Goodbye television. Goodbye, bookshelves. Goodbye table. Goodbye stove. Goodbye bed. Goodbye couch. Goodbye apartment. Goodbye old life. Hello new life.

DOG: Ruff.

15

2:28 PM

(At NIGEL's desk, NIGEL yells at ANNIE as SID strolls by.)

NIGEL: I bet you're proud of yourself! I bet you think that's real funny!

ANNIE: Yes, I do.

SID: What happened?

NIGEL: She glued my keyboard to the desk.

SID: That's pretty funny.

NIGEL: And bolted my chair to the floor.

SID: Really?

NIGEL: So that if I sit in it, I can't reach the keyboard.

SID: Good work.

ANNIE: Thanks.

SID: Why weren't you at your desk?

NIGEL: Because I was at her desk.

ANNIE: My desk? What did you do to my desk? *(Runs to where her desk is... usually)* Where's my desk?!

SID: Classic.

ANNIE: Oh, I am so going to get you.

NIGEL: I welcome it.

ANNIE: I will ruin you.

NIGEL: I will ruin you.

(Exit ANNIE.)

NIGEL: I will ruin you!

(Enter JESSICA, carrying her umbrella.)

SID: Oh good, you're back.

JESSICA: Is it done?

SID: She's here.

ALAN: *(Over at JESSICA's area.)* Okay!

SID: Would you like me to escort you to your cubicle?

(SID holds out his arm for her to take.)

JESSICA: No, I can get there by myself.

(SID and JESSICA walk over to her cubicle. ALAN is already there.)

(Above JESSICA's cubicle they have build a glass ceiling with pieces of colored glass. It's like a stained glass window, except you know, it's a ceiling. It might be rectangular or it might be shaped like a big umbrella. JESSICA looks at it.)

ALAN: What do you think?

SID: Yeah, what do you think?

(JESSICA looks at it.)

ALAN: You always tell that story about your apartment.

SID: And you are always looking up at the ceiling suspiciously.

ALAN: So we thought we would build you a ceiling so that nothing would fall down on you.

SID: It'll protect you.

ALAN: We wanted to protect you.

SID: Do you like it?

JESSICA: I love it.

SID: Oh good, that's great.

JESSICA: It's beautiful.

ALAN: Thank you.

SID: You really like it?

JESSICA: I really do. I should point out though, symbolically, you did put a glass ceiling over the workspace of your female coworker.

ALAN: Oh.

SID: We didn't think of that.

ALAN: We didn't mean it like that.

SID: We're not trying to keep you down.

ALAN: No, we're not. We're trying to beautify your space.

SID: Yeah.

JESSICA: Okay. Well, like I said, it's great.

ALAN: You like it?

JESSICA: Yeah.

SID: Will it make your day better?

JESSICA: I think it will.

ALAN: That's all we want.

JESSICA: It's like art.

SID: Thanks!

ALAN: It's a symbol of our love and admiration.

JESSICA: Oh.

SID: And it also protects you from potentially hazardous things that may or may not fall from the sky.

JESSICA: Cool.

SID: Also, I love you.

JESSICA: What?

SID: Um . . . I mean…

ALAN: Would you like to go out on a date sometime?

SID: With me.

JESSICA: With you or with him?

ALAN: With me.

SID: No, with me.

ALAN: With me, not him.

JESSICA: So you both want to go out on separate dates with me.

SID & ALAN: Yes.

JESSICA: Is that why you built this?

ALAN: No.

SID: Maybe.

JESSICA: I'm really not sure. I like to keep my professional and personal lives separate, you know?

ALAN: I know.

SID: I told you.

JESSICA: On the other hand, you know, that's just a stupid reason not to do things.

ALAN: Agreed.

JESSICA: On the other other hand, it might cause some big problems, between the two of you and between each of you and me. If I date one of you and not the other, jealousy. Or if I date both of you, jealousy. If I break up with one of you, anger. Or, and it's inconceivable, but let's say I had feelings for one of you and you dumped me and then every day I have to see you and be reminded of that pain you caused me over and over. I mean is it worth that?

SID: Yes.

ALAN: Wait, so is it inconceivable that you might have feelings for one of us or that one of us would dump you?

JESSICA: But at the end of the day, really I just have to listen to my heart, you know.

SID: I know.

ALAN: What does your heart say?

(Pause.)

JESSICA: I don't know. I need time to listen to it.

16

2:43 PM

(NIGEL is crouched behind a wall like a tiger ready to pounce. In his hands, a brightly colored machinegun-shaped water gun. ANNIE walks by and he attacks. She screams, but he soaks her. He may even lob a water balloon or two.)

NIGEL: Remember the Alamo! Remember the water cooler and the photocopier and refrigerator!

ANNIE: Is this water?

NIGEL: Yes.

ANNIE: I hate you!

NIGEL: Good.

ANNIE: You are dead to me.

NIGEL: That's fine. Do you bow to me as the superior warrior and call a truce?

ANNIE: No, I do not.

(NIGEL sprays her some more. She screams again.)

ANNIE: That's it. The gloves are off!

NIGEL: Fine!

(ANNIE storms off with as much dignity as she can muster, being that she's soaking wet.)

NIGEL: I'll just wait here for your surrender then!

17

2:58 PM

(SAM on the phone. VIOLET in a spot somewhere.)

SAM: Hello? Hello! Hello!

VIOLET: Hello.

SAM: Oh, good. I thought I lost you. Listen, I've been thinking and I think we should meet tonight.

VIOLET: It's not the right time.

SAM: You say that but how can you know?

VIOLET: It doesn't feel right.

SAM: It feels right to me right now. What if tomorrow is wrong and the day after tomorrow is wronger? What if now is the only time? I don't want to miss our window.

VIOLET: If it's supposed to happen—

SAM: No, I don't believe that. You make it happen yourself. You can't just wait for things to happen. That's no way to live. That's only a partial life. That's a life for ghosts.

VIOLET: I don't know.

SAM: I know. I'm telling you. Everyone is on their own timeline, me, you, your mother and father and I'm telling you my timeline says I need to see you tonight. Will you do it? Will you take life by the balls?

VIOLET: Um—

SAM: Come to my work tonight. Come here and we'll go back to my place and I'll make dinner for you.

VIOLET: I don't know.

SAM: You like spaghetti? I have a two-pot system that's the talk of the town.

VIOLET: It's tempting.

SAM: Wait 'til you taste my sauce. I buy it by the jar. It's got meat in it. It's worth the train ride. I promise.

VIOLET: Sam ...

SAM: Violet ...

VIOLET: I'm sure you make very good pasta.

SAM: The best.

VIOLET: And I look forward to someday tasting it.

SAM: But not tonight.

VIOLET: Not tonight.

SAM: Why?

VIOLET: That's not the right question to ask.

SAM: Why not?

VIOLET: It's not a fair question.

SAM: Why?

VIOLET: I can't.

SAM: Of course you can. There is no reason, no good reason not to come see me. Just come.

VIOLET: I—

SAM: You have to. It's got to be now. Tonight. I don't want to hear an excuse. Don't give me destiny bullshit that only means I don't get to see you. That's not the kind of destiny I believe in. I've never looked forward more to seeing anyone. I've never wanted anything more in my life than I want this. To see you, to touch you, to make you spaghetti and sauce using two pots. It has to be tonight.

VIOLET: But-

SAM: You're allowed to be afraid, but you're not allowed to let your fear keep you from living your life.

VIOLET: I'm not.

SAM: What are you doing?

VIOLET: I'm being sensible. I'm giving my heart space. I'm calming my life down. I'm parceling my romance out in small steps. I'm taking it slow. I'm doing it the right way.

SAM: That's not the way it should be. Falling in love should be like hitting a brick wall. It's unavoidable, sudden and necessary. It can't be controlled. And it's the only way to live your life. Come live with me on the other side of the brick wall.

VIOLET: Well . . .

SAM: No, don't say anything to me except "I'll see you tonight." That's all I can hear. If you say anything else, I won't hear it. And if you refuse me this, I don't think I want to talk to you anymore on the phone. Don't email me. Don't call me. We're beyond that. Either be here at my work tonight or don't ever speak to me again. I'm sorry. That's just the way it has to be. It's how I feel. Be here for me or don't exist to me.

(The spot goes out on VIOLET. She has hung up.)

SAM: Violet? Violet! Hello? Are you there? Shit. *(Pause)* I'm an asshole. *(he tries calling her back. It rings. Her voicemail picks up.)* Hello. If you listen to this message, and I wouldn't blame you if you never listened to this message, please, I'm sorry. Forgive me. I'm an asshole. I'm a foolish asshole. Please call me back. We'll go as fast or as slow as you want. I want it to be right with us. Violet? Please. Please.

18

3:03PM

(DONALD and his CAT in their apartment. DONALD is rubbing a large gun with a rag. It should resemble the squirt gun NIGEL had except it's a real gun. It's probably an Uzi or assault rifle.)

DONALD: Mittens, I hate to admit it, but I'm having doubts. Mittens? I'm not—I don't feel ready. Is there someone I can talk to? Give me someone to talk to. I want to act. I have to act. The time has come. It's … It's –I know it's the right thing to do. And it's now. It has to be now. I just wonder. I have doubts. Dammit, Mittens, I need to talk to someone. Mittens? Mittens? Answer me. Why have you forsaken me?

(CAT does not respond)

DONALD: I know it's the right thing to do at the right time. I know this. I've planned, I've trained. I'm ready for all eventualities, ready to die, aren't I? I'm ready to do what I have to do. But then the doubts come. Give me someone to talk to!!

(CAT does not respond.)

DONALD: You're right. I need to get used to figuring it out by myself. We go through this life alone and we must be prepared to die alone. Even if we are scared. Especially if we are scared. Justice will not exist until I bring it about. The world is unjust and needs a torch bearer to lead the way to a juster world. I can bear the torch. Can't I? Can't I, Mittens?

(CAT does not respond.)

DONALD: Where are the bullets?

19

3:37PM

(ANNIE at her desk, NIGEL at his, trying to unstuck his keyboard.)

ANNIE: Nigel! *(Pause)* Nigel!

NIGEL: What?

ANNIE: I'm transferring a call to you.

NIGEL: Who is it?

ANNIE: I'm transferring now.

(NIGEL's phone rings.)

NIGEL: Who is it?

ANNIE: You better answer it.

NIGEL: Who is it?

ANNIE: Answer it by the third ring or our level of service goes down.

NIGEL: Hello, thank you for calling customer service. This is Nigel. How may I help you? What? Mom? What are you saying?

(ANNIE is over by NIGEL's desk now.)

ANNIE: Oh, right. It's your mom on the phone.

NIGEL: *(on the phone.)* No, that's not true.

ANNIE: I may have told her you're being charged with sexual harassment.

NIGEL: *(on the phone.)* I didn't do anything like that. No, Mom. I wouldn't do that. *(to ANNIE.)* I'm going to get you.

ANNIE: Hold that thought. I have your uncle on hold. I told him you impregnated me and then wouldn't return my calls. Oh and your ex girlfriend might somehow think you're sleeping with her mother.

(ANNIE walks away.)

NIGEL: Which ex girlfriend? Hey! Which ex girlfriend? *(on the phone.)* She's a sick woman, Mom. We're trying to get her help. Listen, I got to go. Right. I know. I know. I have some other calls to make. I don't have time for that story right now. I swear I'm not being fired. I swear. I swear. I didn't harass anyone. She said I did what?! I don't know what that word means. Oohhhh. She said that?! Annie! Annie!!!

20

4:02 PM

(JESSICA's desk. JESSICA works. SID and ALAN enter and lurk. After a while, JESSICA senses their presence and looks up.)

JESSICA: What?

SID: We were just wondering. Alan thought you might have made up your mind by now.

ALAN: We don't want to put pressure on you.

SID: Actually, he does. I suggested we not pressure you but he said let's go ask her. I thought it was a bad idea but I didn't want him to go over alone.

JESSICA: You're not going to let me alone until I decide are you?

ALAN & SID: No.

(JESSICA thinks.)

JESSICA: Okay.

ALAN: Okay what?

JESSICA: Okay, I will go on a date with you.

ALAN: With me?

SID: How come with him?

JESSICA: With both of you.

ALAN: Together?

JESSICA: Separately, like a sane person.

SID: Like a sane person, Alan.

JESSICA: Email me and we'll set the dates up, okay?

SID: You've made me the happiest man in the world.

ALAN: I'll make you the happiest woman in the world.
    You see what I did? You came off like a dick.

JESSICA: Okay, we done here?

ALAN & SID: Yes.

(They start to leave.)

SID: Okay, but who wins now? Whoever sleeps with her
    first?

JESSICA: You both won. Hurray! You both won. Can't
    you be happy with that?

SID: Okay, but one of us won more than the other, right.

ALAN: Dude, wait and see how the date goes.

SID: It just doesn't feel right to me unless there is a clear
    loser and winner.

JESSICA: Alan won.

SID: He did?

JESSICA: Yeah.

SID: But we're still going on a date?

JESSICA: Yeah.

SID: So I still have the opportunity to win in part two?

JESSICA: Sure.

(As SID and ALAN exit)

SID: Sweet. I am going to kick your ass with this date. You don't even know.

ALAN: Go ahead and try it.

21

4:03 PM

(KAREN and DOG sing a hobo song. After the first stanza they are joined by more hobos—the rest of the cast.)

KAREN & DOG:
We're on the hobo road
We follow the hobo code
We carry the hobo load
We sing in the hobo mode

HOBOS:
Wherever a hobo goes
He knows what a hobo knows
He walks on his hobo toes
And smells with his hobo nose

We yell at the hobo crows
With all of our hobo bros
We wash our hobo clothes
And drink from our hobo hose

We dance a hobo dance
In our silly hobo pants
We stand in a hobo stance
And chant our hobo chants

We're looking for hobo grants
We're ranting our hobo rants
Give us a hobo chance
Don't give us no hobo can'ts

(They divide into 3 groups and sing it again as a round. Then one more time all together.)

Cause

We're on the hobo road
We follow the hobo code
We carry the hobo load
We sing in the hobo mode

Wherever a hobo goes
He knows what a hobo knows
He walks on his hobo toes
And smells with his hobo nose

We yell at the hobo crows
With all of our hobo bro's
We wash our hobo clothes
And drink from our hobo hose

We dance a hobo dance
In our silly hobo pants
We stand in a hobo stance
And chant our hobo chants

We're looking for hobo grants
We're ranting our hobo rants
Give us a hobo chance
Don't give us no hobo can'ts

(Hobos can play accompanying musical instruments or even bang on pans if they wish. Or just sing. It should be full of joy and freedom and be an idealized vision of homelessness. The HOBOS leave the DOG and KAREN at the end of the song but they keep singing.)

KAREN: Don't give us no hobo can'ts
Don't give us no hobo can'ts

22

4:15 PM

(NIGEL and ANNIE are shouting at each other. Everyone else is around. Some of them are watching.)

NIGEL: That's my mom. You don't fuck with a guy's mom. That's sacred.

ANNIE: That will teach you to fuck with my desk. My desk is sacred.

NIGEL: You are such a waste of space.

ANNIE: You are a meat head.

NIGEL: Bitch!

ANNIE: Cunt!

NIGEL: *(Pushes her.)* Troll!

ANNIE: *(Shoves him back.)* Moron!

NIGEL: Sociopath!

(They shove each other a couple more times and then AN-NIE throws him down and they start wrestling on the floor. They shout and grunt while wrestling and then DONALD enters carrying his machine gun.)

(DONALD shoots up in the air. The glass ceiling shatters and rains over everyone. It continues to shower them with colored glass, or something like glass anyway. Everyone

hits the ground. ANNIE goes flat on top of NIGEL, shielding him. SID and ALAN both try to pull JESSICA down to safety. Then it's over. There is a silence.)

DONALD: Did I hit anybody?

(EVERYONE stares at him.)

(Just then, VIOLET enters. DONALD's back is to her and she doesn't see the gun.)

VIOLET: Hello? Sam?

SAM: Get out of here! Now's not a good time.

VIOLET: But, you said . . .

SAM: It's just not a good time! Go!!

(VIOLET exits.)

SAM: Shit.

DONALD: Where's Karen?

(Pause)

SID: She's out sick.

DONALD: I kind of thought she'd be here.

ALAN: Are you going to put the gun down?

DONALD: *(Dropping his gun.)* Sorry. Is everyone okay?

(SID grabs the gun, moves away from DONALD quickly locks it in someone's desk)

ANNIE: You were just shooting at us. Why were you shooting at us?

DONALD: I don't know.

ALAN: Dude, the job is not that good. It's not worth shooting anyone over.

DONALD: No?

SAM: No.

DONALD: No.

NIGEL: Should we call the cops?

SID: Are you going to come back again and shoot at us like tomorrow or something?

DONALD: I didn't really shoot at you. It was kind of up in the air. I thought I was going to shoot at you. But then I came in and I didn't do that.

SID: Why not?

ALAN: Don't ask him that!

DONALD: I don't know why not. I thought I would be a hero who the world would celebrate somehow for coming in here and killing you all.

ANNIE: Why did you think that?

DONALD: I'm not really sure why. I lost the why. I don't want to shoot people. Why did I ever think I wanted to shoot people? You ever feel like you know something for certain and then in an instant you're not so certain? Suddenly I feel like I don't know anything. The ground shifted underneath me. Now I don't know where I am. I think my cat may have led me astray. I have to go home and rework my whole manifesto. Maybe get a new cat. Or you know, take my medication again.

SID: But you're not going to come back and do it again?

DONALD: You want to send me to jail? You should probably send me to jail.

SID: You're not going to come back tomorrow with another gun.

DONALD: No.

SID: Promise?

DONALD: Yeah. Sorry. Sorry, everybody. I made a mistake.

ANNIE: That was quite a fucking mistake.

SAM: Come on. Help me figure out your filing system.

(SAM and DONALD exit. ALAN and SID help JESSICA pick up the pieces of her glass ceiling.)

ALAN: Did you get hit by any glass?

JESSICA: I think I'm fine.

SID: You sure?

JESSICA: I'm fine.

NIGEL: You shielded me. When he came in. You protected me from the gunfire.

ANNIE: No I didn't. I was just on top.

NIGEL: You saved my life.

ANNIE: No, that's silly. Don't be silly.

NIGEL: Don't call me silly.

ANNIE: Then stop saying silly things.

NIGEL: You're such a bitch.

ANNIE: Asshole!

(They are in each others' faces and then they are kissing. They are really going at it.)

ALAN: I'm really sorry the ceiling didn't protect you.

SID: We really thought it would.

ALAN: It became the thing that was falling instead of the thing that protected you from things falling.

JESSICA: It's okay. I wasn't directly under it. I'm fine.

ALAN: I just feel terrible.

JESSICA: Things fall, you know? Sometimes things fall.
Things happen beyond our control sometimes. I guess
I should come to terms with that.

SID: We can build you another one.

JESSICA: No, don't. I should live without it.

ALAN: Okay.

SID: So do you like skating? I was thinking on our date
we could go skating.

JESSICA: Oh. Yeah, I don't think I want to go out on a
date with you.

ALAN: Ha!

JESSICA: With either of you.

ALAN: Oh.

SID: But—

JESSICA: I don't like you. Either of you. I mean I don't
dislike you, but let's face it, it's just not going to happen with us.

SID: Was it the glass falling on you?

JESSICA: No, no. It's not anything like that. Life is too
short, you know, to pretend. The fact is there isn't anything you can do or say that's going to make me like
you guys. It's just not happening.

ALAN: Well, that sucks.

ANNIE: You want to come back to my place tonight and I'll make you dinner?

NIGEL: Sounds good.

ANNIE: You like tofu?

NIGEL: Love it.

(They kiss some more.)

(Enter SUE, in police uniform, gun drawn.)

SUE: There was a report of some gunshots. Were there gunshots in here?

ALAN:	SID:
No.	Yeah.

ALAN: There were some gunshots but now, he's gone. The shooter left.

(ALAN looks around to see if the others will go along. They affirm with subtle signals. SUE holsters her gun.)

SUE: Is anyone injured?

(EVERYONE adlibs that they are okay.)

SUE: Did you see where he went?

(EVERYONE adlibs that they don't know.)

SUE: I'm going to have to take statements from all of you.

(SAM and DONALD return from the filing area.)

SAM: Oh.

ALAN: Sam, Donald, welcome. I was just telling the officer here that there was a shooter, shooting but he has gone and we don't know where he went.

DONALD: Oh.

SAM: Yeah, okay.

SUE: Can you describe the shooter?

(SUE moves around writing on her pad as people talk.)

SID: He was a tall man.

ALAN: No, he was short and squat, like a beach ball.

ANNIE: His face was squinty.

NIGEL: His nose was very pointy.

JESSICA: He was oddly handsome in a seen-it-all kind of way.

SID: He was wearing orange.

ALAN: Red.

JESSICA: Black.

NIGEL: White.

JESSICA: He reminded me of my uncle.

NIGEL: He was greasy. He may have been a mechanic or possibly worked in an oil refinery.

ANNIE: Olive oil, you mean. He was covered in the stuff.

SAM: He seemed lost.

SID: He may have been blind.

JESSICA: I think he was on something like PCP or Angel Dust or Crystal Meth.

NIGEL: He had a gigantic wart on his nose that seemed to cover his whole face.

ANNIE: He looked like a pederast.

SID: He came in and shot and then left. Just like that.

ALAN: We all dived down and covered our heads like they say you should do.

SID: I was going to stand in a doorway but then I remembered that's for earthquakes.

DONALD: At the end of the day, when the shit goes down, it turns out I'm not who I thought I was. And that makes me sad. I mean it's important to know, but I want to be the kind of person that starts a revolution not the kind of person that doesn't. I don't know. I'm going to need to go home and talk to my cat. If she's still there, that is.

ANNIE: Something like this makes you think about what you know about yourself, your likes and dislikes, your way in the world. I feel like all this time the things I disliked were really the things I liked and possibly vice versa. I'm not sure what that means except I might be in love.

NIGEL: I might be in love too. I feel like I've been wearing dark glasses all this time and this afternoon, someone knocked them off my face and I can see all the colors of the world that were hiding before and dammit if I want to be a part of everything. And I want to make love.

ANNIE: Yeah.

NIGEL: I haven't had a good fuck in I can't remember how long.

JESSICA: Me either.

SID: Oh come on.

ALAN: Seriously? I'm right here.

JESSICA: Everything is not about the two of you, and your bets and side bets, your tantrums, your proposals, your lust and your desires. I can have desires and you don't have to enter into them in any way. I can have sex dreams and sex day dreams and they can be about someone else. I'm tired of being tied down or covered up. I am not a statue on a pedestal or a flower in a vase. I am not just a beautiful thing, although I am that for sure. But I want to be recognized for who I am, not only how I look.   (continued)

JESSICA (Cont'd): I don't want to always be protected from the world by other people. You don't have to build a ceiling over me. I don't need it. I don't know. Treat me like a normal person, not the freak in the room who happens to be incredibly incredibly beautiful.

SID: I guess.

SAM: You know what? If you excuse me, I think I have to go chase down a girl. I'll see you all tomorrow.

ALAN: See you tomorrow.

(SAM exits.)

SID: Lucky bastard.

ALAN: Yeah. He's lucky. I don't feel unlucky exactly.

SID: I guess I don't either.

ALAN: Not in any large way.

SID: There have been setbacks.

ALAN: Sure.

SID: I watch people get lucky or whatever and fly by me.

ALAN: It was their time.

SID: Was it? They have houses and kids and stable jobs. Gardens, dogs.

ALAN: Children.

SID: Dogs.

ALAN: They save their money.

SID: They drive nice cars.

ALAN: Their wives are beautiful.

SID: Their lives are beautiful.

ALAN: Beautiful houses. All that anyone could want in the world.

SID: Do you want that?

ALAN: I just want someone to give me a shot.

SID: Yeah.

ALAN: Try me out. There are lots of things I can do.

SID: You don't even know.

ALAN: Look at me.

SID: I got a lot going on.

ALAN: I could be somebody.

SID: If you just let me.

ALAN: Just let me.

SID: They should let us.

ALAN: Yeah.

DONALD: I feel forgotten too.

SID: Sure.

DONALD: I'm not sure what to do next.

ALAN: You wake up tomorrow morning.

SID: Right.

ALAN: And then do something.

SID: Something new.

ALAN: Something new.

DONALD: Okay.

SID: Something sane.

SUE: Well thank you all. I don't know that that will help me catch the perp per se but I do feel like we're getting somewhere. Everyday, we try to get somewhere new. That's the way I try to live my life and it's working out so far. I mean, don't get me wrong. It's not perfect. My life is not ideal.

I used to be an addict. It burned down a lot of bridges behind me. There are a lot of people who won't talk to me anymore though I wish they would. I'm not telling you this because I want your sympathy. (continued)

SUE (Cont'd): Or pity. I'm just a person. I went through something and came out the other side, scarred but intact. And there is temptation of course everyday but I tell myself, that was a bad life I led. And I embraced the law and what is good and right because it seemed like the opposite way was the way to go, you know?

People can change.

DONALD: I know.

SUE: Most people don't. But they can. You can go to God. That works for some people. Or shrinks or I don't know. We all have our own paths. But I think it's important to make sure you're on the right path for you, you know? Look at where you're going. Get out of the car, examine the map, make plans if you can. But don't just put your foot down on the gas and shoot down the highway in the fast lane without proper consideration of where the fuck you're going.

JESSICA: Yeah.

SUE: *(To JESSICA.)* But really I guess what I want to say is would you like to go out sometime?

JESSICA: Me?

SUE: Oh, I'm sorry, did I misread the situation?

JESSICA: Well.

SUE: I'm sorry. I always do this. I'm inventing connections.

JESSICA: No.

SUE: I'm not?

JESSICA: Well.

SUE: Forget I said anything.

JESSICA: It's just, I've never gone out on a date with a girl.

SUE: I thought that might be the case. So ...

JESSICA: Let's do it.

SUE: Really?

JESSICA: Why not?

SID: Oh, come on!

ALAN: I call gender discrimination!

JESSICA: Don't mind them.

(The phone rings. SID answers it.)

SID: Thank you for calling customer service.

(MR. HENDERSON enters. He is imposing.)

MR. HENDERSON: What's going on here?

ANNIE: Mr. Henderson. We didn't know you were coming to see us today.

MR. HENDERSON: It's a surprise. Surprise! What happened here?

SUE: There was a shooting.

MR. HENDERSON: A what?

SUE: The perp escaped. No injuries.

MR. HENDERSON: What's all this glass?

ALAN: Oh, that was a glass ceiling Sid and I built.

MR. HENDERSON: What for?

ALAN: Um . . .

MR. HENDERSON: No more glass ceilings.

ANNIE: Here, here!

MR. HENDERSON: *(To DONALD.)* Do you still work here?

SID: He was showing us the filing system, weren't you?

DONALD: Yeah.

MR. HENDERSON: Where's Karen?

ANNIE: She's been out all week. We thought you knew.

MR. HENDERSON: What the hell's going on here?

(No one says anything.)

MR. HENDERSON: Fine. That's fine. All right. Everything's going to go back to normal. Normal is always the best thing. I'll call Karen in. I'll right all wrongs. I'll solve all problems. That's my job. I'm the boss. I'm firm, but kind. You like that don't you? Of course you do. Why doesn't everyone take the rest of the day off?

(EVERYONE starts to leave. JESSICA picks up her umbrella, opens it. She changes her mind, hands the open umbrella to MR. HENDERSON, then she exits too.)

SID: *(has been on the phone.)* Okay. Goodbye. I love you.

(SID makes eye contact with MR. HENDERSON and he exits too. MR. HENDERSON is alone on stage)

MR. HENDERSON: Unbelievable. Why do I keep doing this?

(He makes a phone call.)

(Meanwhile, KAREN and the DOG stand before the bridge.)

KAREN: Are you ready? Are you ready to cross this bridge out of Manhattan into a new life?

DOG: I think so. Yes. Ruff.

(Then her phone rings. It rings and rings and rings. She looks at it. Blackout.)

(END OF PLAY)

More Plays Available From
Original Works Publishing

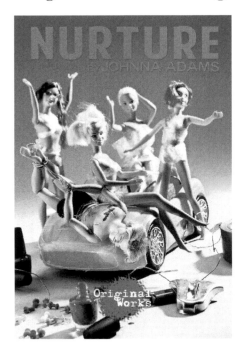

<u>NURTURE</u> by Johnna Adams

Synopsis: Doug and Cheryl are horrible single parents drawn together by their equally horrible daughters. The star-crossed parental units journey from first meeting to first date, to first time, to first joint parent-teacher meeting, to proposal and more. They attempt to form a modern nuclear family while living in perpetual fear of the fruit of their loins and someone abducting young girls in their town.

Cast Size: 1 Male, 1 Female

<u>MITZI'S ABORTION</u> by Elizabeth Heffron

Synopsis: With humor, intelligence and honesty, *Mitzi's Abortion* explores the questions that have shaped the national debate over abortion, and reminds us that whatever we may think we believe, some decisions are neither easy nor simple when they become ours to make. A generous and compassionate comedy with serious themes about a young woman trying to make an intensely personal decision in a system determined to make it a political one.

Cast Size: 4 Males, 3 Female

93

OWL MOON by Liz Maestri

Synopsis: What happens when an Owl Moon rises? The everyday world veers into extremities – hot blood spurts and passions seep into a wintry landscape of cold and desolation. Two couples venture into a desolate, frozen snowfield for the night where they find themselves trapped, both physically and in the mire of their own neurosis. Lisa is determined to win back her ex, Isaac, and will stop at nothing to do so. Shell and Salome carry weighty sacks across the snow, looking for a way to purge their sins. The play follows this group of characters through conflicts and collisions that stretch taut conventions of style and tone. Is it possible to lose oneself? To lose oneself in another? Owl Moon examines the fine line between passion and obsession, and the toll it takes on the mind and spirit. Add in a talking owl, and you have a play that juggles the heady, humorous and harrowing in equal measure.

Cast Size: 1 Male, 3 Females, 1 Talking Owl

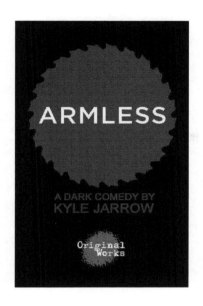

ARMLESS by Kyle Jarrow

Synopsis: John is a normal man, except for one thing: he wants his arms cut off. John suffers from Body Integrity Disorder, a psychological condition in which an individual paradoxically doesn't feel "whole" unless he loses one or more major limbs. When John attempts to find a doctor willing to perform this operation, it triggers a twisted romp filled with mistaken identities, missed chances, and tragic consequences. This provocative farce by OBIE Award winner Kyle Jarrow explores our notions of personal freedom and medical ethics. It's a darkly funny, strangely poignant tale of love, lies, and amputation.

Cast Size: 2 Males, 2 Females

NOTES

NOTES

NOTES

NOTES

5118235R00056

Made in the USA
San Bernardino, CA
24 October 2013